Christmas

MEMORIES

preserving family histories

———

WRITTEN BY KAREN CULOS

ILLUSTRATED BY

MARIA MIRANDA LAWRENCE AND LINDA LEADBETTER

Quail Publishing
3711 Epsom Drive
Victoria, B.C. V8P 3S8

Canadian Cataloguing in Publication Data
Culos, Karen, 1962-
Christmas memories

Includes bibliographical references.
ISBN 0-9684364-0-4

1. Christmas. 2. Diaries (Blank-books).
I. Lawrence, Maria Miranda, 1953-   II. Leadbetter, Linda, 1959- III. Title.
GT4985.C84 1998   394.2663   C98-910998-4

Designed by Donna Jay
Printed and bound in Canada by Friesen Printers
Printed on acid-free, recycled paper

Acknowledgements

I AM VERY THANKFUL to all the people who have supported or encouraged me to create *Christmas Memories*. There are a few people whose assistance I feel especially blessed to have had on this wonderful journey.

I am deeply grateful to Daniel Goodenough who first encouraged me to create this book and then helped me stay with it when my resolve faltered. I am also deeply grateful to Kimberly Goodenough for being a living example of love and joy, and reminding me of the Christmas Spirit.

I am very grateful to Kathleen Hamilton for her meticulous yet sensitive editing of this book while teaching and encouraging me to strive for more as a writer.

My heartfelt gratitude goes to the creative team who helped me bring this book to print. I wish to thank Maria Lawrence for her total dedication to this project. I am touched by the thought, love and care that went into each watercolour painting. I thank Linda Leadbetter for coming out of retirement to face that first anxious pencil line and add her special touches to this book. Her enthusiasm was contagious. I am thankful to Donna Jay for taking the intangible dream and vision that lived within my heart and creating tangible beauty with it. I am awed and inspired by this. It has been an honour to work with each of these three women.

Throughout this process a number of people have supported me with kind words, encouragement, patience with our schedules and technical advice. I greatly appreciate this support from the Lawrence family, the Leadbetter family, Fran Aitkens, Joan McAnally, and Earl and Jean Schmidt.

My deepest gratitude goes to my family, without whom this book would not have been possible. I am very thankful for the many Christmases we have had together, for the love and laughter, and the memories we created. I am grateful to my father for helping bring my mother's creativity and visions to life, to produce those magical childhood Christmases. I deeply appreciate his continued love, support and faith in me. I thank my brother for sharing the joy and magic of Christmas with his little sister and for the music we created.

Finally, I wish to thank my husband Mark for his love and support through the years. I greatly appreciate his advice, encouragement and patience with this creative process. I am truly grateful for the life we share and I look forward to creating new Christmas memories.

FOR MY MOTHER

_____

who taught me
about love, celebration,
the Spirit of Christmas,
and the magic of the season,
with love and gratitude.

From My Home To Yours

Season's Greetings

CHRISTMAS IS TRULY a wonderful time of year, with the many glorious sights and sounds. The mention of Christmas evokes so many different images and sensations for me. I remember the excitement of the first snowfall and the exhilaration of skating on a frozen pond. I recall the beauty of lights twinkling on houses at dusk, an artfully crafted nativity scene, brightly wrapped presents and a lovingly decorated tree with lights shining through fragrant needles. I breathe in the aromas of shortbread baking and turkey roasting. I hear the uplifting sounds of joyful Christmas carols and the laughter of children as they make snow angels and snowmen. I reminisce about celebratory gatherings with family and friends. And I feel a sense of peace as a child's gaze is held by an elegant angel or cherished ornament. These are some of the images that mean Christmas to me.

Christmas is also a time when people are kinder to one another, friends and strangers alike. It is a time when people will give up a seat for a weary fellow passenger, help someone in need or make an extra effort for a friend or neighbour. It is a time when we experience the Christmas Spirit, the love, joy, beauty, and celebration that live in all of us.

This book has been created to help you capture and preserve the Christmas Spirit as you experience it. It is a place to record your own stories, the images that touch your heart and the memories that bring you joy. For each year there are blank pages and suggested topics to write about. This book is yours to use as creatively as you wish. You may choose to draw, paint, make a collage, add photos or other mementoes. You may decide to have only one person write in the book, or you may want to make it a collection of stories and comments by family and friends. Whatever direction your creative spirit takes, enjoy the process as you preserve the magical moments of the season.

May your life be blessed by the Christmas Spirit all year long.

Karen

May the
light and love
of the Christmas Spirit
fill your hearts and
shine in your life
always.

Christmas

MEMORIES

of

_____

spanning the years

_____ *to* _____

THE HISTORY OF THE
Poinsettia

ACCORDING TO Mexican legend, people would lay gifts next to the church altar on Christmas Eve to honour the Holy birth. One little boy, having no money to buy a gift, knelt in prayer to the infant Christ. A miracle resulted from his prayers and a beautiful red and green flower grew where he knelt. He presented this to the altar and it became known as the first Flower of the Holy Night.

Dr. Joel Poinsett, the American ambassador to Mexico from 1825 to 1829, was very interested in this plant. When he returned to America he took one with him. The Flower of the Holy Night became a popular Christmas plant and was renamed "Poinsettia" after Dr. Poinsett.✽

Christmas
MEMORIES

_____

YEAR

Family & Friends
Who Visited

_____   _____

_____   _____

_____   _____

_____   _____

_____   _____

_____   _____

_____   _____

_____   _____

_____   _____

People We Visited

FAMILY AND FRIENDS

photo

Christmas Eve

The sights, sounds, tastes and celebrations

Christmas Day

How We Spent Our Day

_____
_____
_____
_____
_____
_____
_____
_____

Who We Shared Christmas Dinner With

_____
_____
_____
_____

OUR FAVOURITE RECIPE

What Was Served

_____
_____
_____
_____
_____
_____
_____
_____
_____

Our Home For The Holidays

_____

_____

_____

_____

_____

_____

_____

_____

photo

OUR DECORATED HOME

What Touched Our Hearts

Sights, sounds, events, people

Special Gifts

What We Want To Remember
Memorable moments, future celebrations

A MEMORABLE MOMENT

_____

_____

_____

_____

_____

_____

_____

_____

_____

_____

_____

Favourite Memories of Family and Friends

_____

_____

_____

_____

_____

_____

_____

_____

Christmas

These pages
are yours to use
as creatively as
you wish.

Memories

The Stockings Were Hung With Care

ONE YEAR my friend Lisa and her three brothers felt extremely pressured at the thought of buying Christmas gifts. Time and money were scarce. Each of them was either writing university finals or had just become a parent. Christmas was becoming a burden rather than a joyful celebration.

Lisa and her brothers told their parents how they felt. They all agreed that what was most important to them was spending time together, so they decided against the large gift exchange that year. Instead, they would fill Christmas stockings for each other with small gifts, purchased or handmade, costing no more than five dollars. Each person would supply his or her own stocking to hold these wrapped items. Everyone breathed a deep sigh of relief. The whole family became excited and enthusiastic about Christmas. Their imaginations and creativity were sparked by the image of what might emerge from the stockings Christmas morning.

On Christmas Eve three generations — with ages ranging from four months to sixty-two years — gathered under one roof. Anticipation and excitement filled the air. Each person placed their stocking in the living room before going to bed. In the morning they all paused, wide-eyed, as they entered the living room. It was neither the family-decorated tree glowing with lights nor the snow softly falling outside that caught their attention. It was the stockings! Seventeen multicoloured, multipatterned stockings, all shapes and sizes, bulging in interesting ways, hung around the fireplace mantle.

Everyone was given their own stocking to open as they chose. Some tore through the wrapping paper in a frenzy of excitement. Others went slowly, carefully unwrapping each package, savouring the moment. For a while, "oohs," "aahs" and laughter were all that could be heard.

Afterwards Lisa and her family enjoyed just being together, grateful that family togetherness was the new focus of their Christmas holiday. Delighted by their experience, they made family gatherings with Christmas stockings their new tradition. Even now, many years later, they continue to celebrate Christmas this same way: simply, with love and togetherness.

After starting this custom in my own family, I awakened my Christmas Spirit through the simple act of opening stockings. It reconnected me to a time of innocence and simple pleasures, to the joy of celebration and the excitement of hidden treasures. I was once again looking at Christmas through the eyes of a child. ✳

Christmas
MEMORIES

Family & Friends
Who Visited

_____ _____

_____ _____

_____ _____

_____ _____

_____ _____

_____ _____

_____ _____

_____ _____

_____ _____

People We Visited

_____

_____

_____

_____

_____

_____

_____

Christmas Eve

The sights, sounds, tastes and celebrations

_____

_____

_____

_____

_____

_____

_____

_____

Christmas Day

How We Spent Our Day

_____
_____
_____
_____
_____
_____
_____
_____

Who We Shared Christmas Dinner With

_____
_____
_____
_____

OUR FAVOURITE RECIPE

What Was Served

_____
_____
_____
_____
_____
_____
_____
_____
_____
_____

Our Home For The Holidays

_____

_____

_____

_____

_____

_____

_____

_____

_____

photo

OUR DECORATED HOME

What Touched Our Hearts

Sights, sounds, events, people

_____

_____

_____

_____

_____

Special Gifts

_____

_____

_____

_____

_____

What We Want To Remember
Memorable moments, future celebrations

A MEMORABLE MOMENT

_____

_____

_____

_____

_____

_____

_____

_____

_____

_____

_____

Favourite Memories of Family and Friends

_____

_____

_____

_____

_____

_____

_____

Christmas

*These pages
are yours to use
as creatively as
you wish.*

Memories

The
Season
of Dreams

What a gift it is
to have the opportunity to make
one of our dreams come true. So many times we overlook
these opportunities in the busyness of our lives
or we have forgotten our dreams.

LAST YEAR our family decided to spend Christmas together in Banff. Some of the family already lived there and there was plenty of room for out-of-town guests. It would be the first time we had all spent Christmas together in many years.

As I shopped and packed with anticipation, I thought of my long-time dream of spending Christmas in a small snow-covered town, the kind you might see on a postcard. My dream image was of tall evergreens laden with snow, a small church and charming shops lining Main Street, windows and roof-tops outlined with glowing lights, bright blue skies, lightly falling snow, and a friendly atmosphere. My husband Mark and I would be outside enjoying the fresh clean air, knowing that a cozy fire waited to warm us after our walk. This image has been with me for many years. Christmas with my family in Banff could fulfil this dream.

As we drove from the Calgary airport to Banff on the evening of the twenty-third, I slept until we neared the entrance to Banff National Park. As if I had heard a bell, I woke up. I wasn't about to miss the first opportunity to see the town of my dreams! As we approached Banff, tiny lights began to glint among the trees like fireflies. Then more and more lights appeared. Soon the shapes of buildings emerged from the darkness, as tiny white twinkling lights outlined each resort. Between the buildings, the dark trees dotted with white lights looked stunning.

The view of the town was magical! We saw shop windows decorated for the holidays, coloured lights outlining rooftops, a quaint church on a street corner, decorations in the central boulevard, trees glowing with tiny white lights, and late-night shoppers enjoying the clean crisp air. A light snow began to fall as we drove through the town. How perfect!

The next day Mark and I explored the downtown area, bundled up against the crisp mountain air. It felt cold after living on the balmy West Coast for many years. We browsed, looked in windows and enjoyed the energetic, holiday atmosphere. The rest of our relatives arrived that afternoon and the festivities began. The long oak table was covered with a white tablecloth and a red table runner. Evergreen boughs and candles were placed along it. In the living room candles glowed, a fire crackled in the stone fireplace, and the decorated Christmas tree was circled with gifts. Behind the tree, the large expanse of picture windows framed the moonlit trees and the lightly falling snow.

We had three days of joyous family celebration. We talked, shared meals, opened Christmas gifts, walked in the snow and relaxed together. On our last day, I walked downtown to watch the changing light in the night sky and breathe in the fragrant air. A wintertime sky at dusk has a special colour and depth to it, and the air a quality that makes everything seem possible. As I took one more breath of this magical night air, I looked around at the lights, decorations, and people — all the things that were part of my dream.

Mark and I journeyed home, cocooned in the warmth and love of our Christmas experience. As I reflected, I realized I was doubly blessed. Another long-time dream had become a reality: the dream of having a large family gathering once again. With joy and gratitude I hold these memories in my heart. In this season of love, magic and dreams, may yours come true this year.✻

Christmas
MEMORIES

_____

YEAR

Family & Friends
Who Visited

_____ _____

_____ _____

_____ _____

_____ _____

_____ _____

_____ _____

_____ _____

_____ _____

People We Visited

_____

_____

_____

_____

_____

_____

_____

photo

FAMILY AND FRIENDS

Christmas Eve

The sights, sounds, tastes and celebrations

_____

_____

_____

_____

_____

_____

_____

Christmas Day

How We Spent Our Day

_____

_____

_____

_____

_____

_____

_____

_____

Who We Shared Christmas Dinner With

_____

_____

_____

_____

What Was Served

_____

_____

_____

_____

_____

_____

_____

_____

OUR FAVOURITE RECIPE

Our Home For The Holidays

_____

_____

_____

_____

_____

_____

_____

_____

OUR DECORATED HOME

What Touched Our Hearts
Sights, sounds, events, people

_____

_____

_____

_____

_____

Special Gifts

_____

_____

_____

_____

_____

What We Want To Remember
Memorable moments, future celebrations

A MEMORABLE MOMENT

_____

_____

_____

_____

_____

_____

_____

_____

_____

_____

_____

Favourite Memories of Family and Friends

_____

_____

_____

_____

_____

_____

_____

_____

_____

Christmas

Memories

THE HISTORY OF

Santa Claus

MID-WINTER HAS TRADITIONALLY
BEEN A TIME FOR EXCHANGING GIFTS.

THE CHURCH, finding gift-giving such a popular pagan custom, decreed that gifts were to be given in honour of the Infant Jesus. Each country chose its own gift bringers. In Spain, it was the Three Kings; in Italy, Befana, a kind old woman on a broomstick; in Russia, Babouschka, a grandmotherly figure; and in Germany, Christkind or Christ Child, an angelic messenger from Jesus. In Scandinavia, gifts were delivered by gnomes or nisser who had no sinister qualities, only the Christmas Spirit. And in many other countries it was Santa Claus.

Today, in most countries where Christmas is celebrated, a red-robed, white-bearded figure distributes gifts some time between December 5th and January 6th. In North America, we call him Santa Claus and sometimes refer to him as St. Nick. The original St. Nicholas, an early 4th century bishop of Myra, was considered the patron saint of children and unmarried girls. Many stories are told about him, the most common being that he generously provided dowries for three daughters of a poor nobleman. One story says that when he threw the bags of gold into the house they landed in a stocking hung to dry by the fire, another says he dropped the bags down a chimney and they came to rest in a shoe or stocking. Either way, this is how the custom of hanging Christmas stockings by the fireplace originated.

After St. Nicholas' death, December 6th became St. Nicholas Day. On St. Nicholas Eve, a tall, thin man in full Episcopal dress of red and white vestments, gold embroidered cape, mitre and staff would go through town rewarding children for good behaviour and threatening punishment for bad behaviour. In some areas, St. Nicholas was accompanied by a monster whose job it was to carry out the punishment, and in other areas by an angel who represented the better St. Nicholas. In some areas the one figure that arrived was a composite of St. Nicholas and the monster. Children were taught to fear this figure. *Continued next page.*

In Northern Europe today, your gifts will be brought by gnomes; in Italy, by Befana; in Spain, by the Three Kings; in Russia, by Grandfather Frost; and in Germany, by the Christ Child.

EARLY DUTCH settlers brought Sint Nicholaas or Sinterklaas to America. They dedicated the first church built in New Amsterdam, now New York City, to him. The English later adopted him in the 17th century and anglicized his name to Santa Claus. After the Protestant Reformation in Europe, many countries rejected St. Nicholas as "too Popish."

In the 18th century, German and German-speaking Swiss immigrants brought the Christ Child to America. Over time their version of a child on a mule laden with presents was transformed into Kriss Kringle. By the middle of the 19th century he was being confused with Santa Claus or St. Nicholas. The final merging of St. Nicholas, the bishop of Myra, with Santa Claus occurred with Dr. Clement Clarke Moore's poem, written in 1822 for his children. "A Visit From St. Nicholas" was published a year later when a guest, after hearing it, anonymously sent the poem to the *Troy Sentinel*. Although many illustrations were drawn of St. Nicholas for this poem, it was *Harper's Weekly* illustrator Thomas Nast who drew a large jovial image and gave him the name "Santa Claus." This image is still with us today.

Many European countries still honour the original customs of gift giving. In Northern Europe today, your gifts will be brought by gnomes; in Italy, by Befana; in Spain, by the Three Kings; in Russia, by Grandfather Frost; and in Germany, by the Christ Child. In Holland, St. Nicholas, often on his white horse accompanied by Black Pete (who keeps the records of children's behaviour), visits hospitals and takes part in parades. Then on St. Nicholas Eve children leave shoes filled with hay or carrots by the fireplace and wake in the morning to find the shoes filled with sweets and small presents. St. Nicholas is also found in some areas of France, Germany, Belgium and Hungary, and many areas of Switzerland hold a parade on St. Nicholas Eve. Although these countries still recognize their traditional gift bringers, the popularity of the North American Santa Claus is finding its way around the world. Many of the traditional gift-giving customs are now being replaced by or celebrated side by side with Santa Claus.❃

Christmas
MEMORIES

_____

YEAR

Family & Friends
Who Visited

_____   _____

_____   _____

_____   _____

_____   _____

_____   _____

_____   _____

_____   _____

_____   _____

_____   _____

People We Visited

_____

_____

_____

_____

_____

_____

_____

FAMILY AND FRIENDS

Christmas Eve

The sights, sounds, tastes and celebrations

Christmas Day

How We Spent Our Day

_____

_____

_____

_____

_____

_____

_____

_____

Who We Shared Christmas Dinner With

_____

_____

_____

_____

What Was Served

_____

_____

_____

_____

_____

_____

_____

_____

OUR FAVOURITE RECIPE

Our Home For The Holidays

_____

_____

_____

_____

_____

_____

_____

_____

_____

OUR DECORATED HOME

What Touched Our Hearts

Sights, sounds, events, people

Special Gifts

_____

_____

_____

_____

_____

_____

What We Want To Remember
Memorable moments, future celebrations

A MEMORABLE MOMENT

_____

_____

_____

_____

_____

_____

_____

_____

_____

_____

_____

Favourite Memories of Family and Friends

_____

_____

_____

_____

_____

_____

_____

_____

Christmas

Memories

Christmas Trees

FIR IS THE WOOD OF PEACE, AND EVERGREEN
IS THE SYMBOL OF CHRIST'S EVERLASTING LIFE.

———

FOR MANY PEOPLE, Christmas would not seem complete without a fragrant evergreen tree decorated with lights and ornaments, surrounded by gifts for family and friends. Evergreens have been used in midwinter celebrations since the Roman times. One legend of the origin of the Christmas tree involves St. Boniface, an 8th century Christian missionary. One Christmas Eve while in Germany, he was so shocked to see a pagan winter festival including sacrifice that he toppled the sacred Oak tree of Odin with one blow. The people were awestruck by this feat and converted to Christianity. When they expressed their sadness at losing their giant tree, St. Boniface pointed to a small fir now growing where the oak tree had stood and said, "Take that as your symbol. Fir is the wood of peace, and evergreen is the symbol of Christ's everlasting life." St. Boniface also said, "Take the tree home, gather around it and celebrate the birth of the Saviour Jesus Christ with songs and ceremonies of love."

The immediate predecessor of today's Christmas tree was called the Paradise tree. This was a fir tree decorated with apples to represent the tree from which Adam and Eve ate against God's wishes, resulting in their expulsion from Paradise. In the Medieval church calendar, December 24th was known as Adam and Eve day. Plays held in Germany on this day depicted the fall of Adam and Eve, with a Paradise tree being the main prop at centre stage. These plays were held to emphasize the birth of Christ, who was considered the second Adam sent to redeem the original. This popular custom of decorating trees found its way into people's homes, where the tree was decorated on Christmas Eve with apples, paper flowers, and white wafers to symbolize Christ.

It is generally agreed that Martin Luther, a 16th century German theologian, was the first person to put candles on a Christmas tree. Walking home one night shortly before Christmas, Luther was moved by the sight of the bright stars twinkling through the dark trees. He deeply felt his connection with God. He hurried home to reproduce for his children the beauty and love he had experienced, by placing candles on an evergreen tree.

The custom of decorating a Christmas tree eventually spread throughout Europe and reached England in 1789. It became popular in the 1840s when Queen Victoria and Prince Albert, her German husband, set up a tree for their children in Windsor Castle. Around this time, the Christmas tree found its way to America.

In 1851, a young Ohio pastor placed a lighted Christmas tree next to a church altar. Believing this to be a pagan practice, the townspeople created an uproar. The pastor had to show them, through much research, that this was a custom in America. Christmas trees soon became a part of both home and church celebrations. Gradually, Christian symbols were introduced and decorations such as angels, crosses, hearts, stars, and golden strands of tinsel were added to give meaning to this custom. The stars represented the star of the East and the tinsel represented the hair of the infant Christ. Lights were later added to represent Christ as the light of the world.

Today, the Christmas tree has become one of the most popular symbols of the Christmas season. The awe-inspiring spectacle of tree, lights, ornaments, angels, stars, candy canes, and tinsel leaves children with memories for years to come.✳

Christmas trees soon became

a part of both home

and church celebrations.

Holly

HOLLY IS STEEPED in superstition and myth because it stayed green and continued to grow while other plants were brown and leafless. It is considered the symbol for good luck and eternal life and it is believed to ward off evil spirits. Traditionally in England prickly-leaved holly is considered "he" and smooth-leaved holly "she". According to English myth whichever type is first brought into the house at Christmas will determine which sex will rule the house the following year.

Ornaments

THE FIRST CHRISTMAS trees were decorated with fruit and flowers; later cookies, nuts, other foods and lighted candles were added. Many tree branches would droop under all this weight. By the late 19th century these heavy ornaments were replaced by featherweight glass balls produced by German glass blowers and light tin ornaments made by German toy makers. This was the beginning of the variety of ornaments seen on trees today (and the end of drooping branches!). In North America, our ornaments usually include balls, stars, tinsel and Santas. Other countries have their own traditional ornaments, such as straw animal figures and wooden ornaments in Sweden, paper hearts and bells in Denmark, paper fans and butterflies in Japan, and painted egg shells in some eastern European countries.

Tree Lights

THE EARLY CHRISTMAS trees decorated with burning candles were quite a fire hazard. Many homes even kept buckets of water near the tree to put out the flames. The variety of lights seen on Christmas trees today began with an idea Ralph E. Morris had in 1895. As an employee of New England Telephone, Morris was looking at the string of lights used in telephone switchboards and thought of using them on his Christmas tree. Once introduced to the public, electric tree lights quickly replaced candles.

Christmas
M E M O R I E S

_____

YEAR

Family & Friends
Who Visited

_____ _____
_____ _____
_____ _____
_____ _____
_____ _____
_____ _____
_____ _____
_____ _____
_____ _____

People We Visited

_____

_____

_____

_____

_____

_____

_____

FAMILY AND FRIENDS

Christmas Eve

The sights, sounds, tastes and celebrations

_____

_____

_____

_____

_____

_____

_____

Christmas Day

How We Spent Our Day

_____

_____

_____

_____

_____

_____

_____

_____

_____

Who We Shared Christmas Dinner With

_____

_____

_____

_____

OUR FAVOURITE RECIPE

What Was Served

_____

_____

_____

_____

_____

_____

_____

_____

_____

Our Home For The Holidays

_____

_____

_____

_____

_____

_____

_____

_____

_____

_____

OUR DECORATED HOME

What Touched Our Hearts

Sights, sounds, events, people

_____

_____

_____

_____

_____

Special Gifts

_____

_____

_____

_____

_____

What We Want To Remember
Memorable moments, future celebrations

A MEMORABLE MOMENT

Favourite Memories of Family and Friends

Christmas

These pages are yours to use as creatively as you wish.

Memories

A Celebration
of the Christmas Spirit

THE FINAL EVENT THAT SIGNIFIED THE ARRIVAL OF CHRISTMAS
WAS THE FAMILY OUTING TO GET A TREE.

―――――――

LIFE OFTEN BRINGS us little treasures and gifts that we are not aware of at the time. So it was with my mother's gift of the Spirit of Christmas. She combined her creativity, her love for her family, and her celebration of life to make Christmas magical for all. She had a way of making the flow of events seem effortless. As a young child I thought everyone had a Christmas like ours, filled with love, warmth, joy and celebration. Now I can see Mom's hand in the many special touches that created those Christmases for us.

In November there were early Christmas events, each one heralding what was to come. First my mother drew our Christmas card, highlighting our year in an image. The card was printed at a local store and my family would gather excitedly to see the first one off the press. They were always beautiful, the image outlined in white on the blue background. Mom wrote a letter inside each card, sending our love to friends and relatives. Next, Christmas desserts were baked and frozen. Traditionally, making sugar cookies was a mother-daughter event. Working together, we made and rolled the cookie dough, cut the Christmas shapes and iced the cooled cookies. What a wonderful afternoon!

The final event that signified the arrival of Christmas was the family outing to get a tree. Everyone had an opinion about which tree was best. After much deliberation the chosen tree was strapped to the roof of our station wagon. Once the tree was secured in its stand in our living room, we began decorating. Out of the Christmas Box came the lights, garlands, coloured balls, angels, stars, handmade ornaments and tinsel. With cries of delight we carefully unwrapped each one and hung it on the tree. When all the empty boxes were put away, we sat in front of the tree and admired our beautiful creation. What a feast for the senses! We revelled in the sound of joyous carols, the sharp scent of evergreen boughs, the sparkle of tinsel, the steam rising from our mugs and the delectable flavour of hot chocolate.

That moment of peace soon gave way to frantic activity as aunts, uncles, and grandparents arrived to stay. My brother and I loved this; there were aunts and uncles to play with us, grandparents to dote on us and people to entertain with our stories and music.

EVERY CHRISTMAS EVE before bed, we set out cookies and milk for Santa, and a carrot for the reindeer. The next morning when Mom and Dad opened the living room doors, my brother and I, still dressed in our pajamas, raced in to see if Santa had been there. He always came. Each year, next to the empty glass and plate we found an elaborate note. Written in rhyming verse, it said we'd been good children and wished us well for the coming year. Unhooking our stockings from the mantle we settled in the middle of the living room floor. From the sofa, our parents watched my brother and me open the tissue-wrapped items and eat the mandarin oranges that Santa always left in the toe of the stocking. Squeals of excitement and laughter rang out with each new discovery. Sometimes Santa even came in person on Christmas morning to deliver a special gift!

After breakfast we opened the gifts piled under the tree. What a sight! Solid green, red and white shapes lay together with boxes wrapped with snowmen and santas. Glittery bows and ribbon sparkled atop these parcels, while solid stripes of color and curly ribbons accented the festive paper. Wrapping these gifts creatively brought Mom great joy as she thought of the person receiving the package, while making each one a thing of beauty. And under the tree or sometimes in another room was a larger item, like a bicycle, a doll house or a train set. They had been kept unassembled, hidden in their boxes until Christmas Eve, because of their size or nature. So, for many years my Dad stayed up very late Christmas Eve, assembling toys for my brother and me.

We ended each Christmas Day with a celebratory dinner and evening of song. Everyone dressed up for the occasion. The table would be elegantly decorated with linens, ornaments, a centrepiece, name tags and crackers. After a wonderful feast the singing began. Mom always played the piano, and depending on who was visiting, there could be violin, guitar, autoharp, cello or harmonica. Everyone sang, rejoicing in the day.

As time went by some of our activities changed, but the essence of Christmas remained the same — the love, joy, togetherness and celebration. One of the changes was that as my brother and I grew older, Mom would wake up earlier than we did on Christmas morning. Faint words would begin to touch me in my sleep, becoming louder, finally waking me. It was my mother. Full of excitement and anticipation, she was saying to Dad, "Do you think they're up yet?"

Throughout our years together, my Mom, with my Dad's help, gave my brother and me the opportunity to believe in dreams and the Spirit of Christmas. No one knew then that we would have so few years together. Mom left us the gift of her love for Christmas and the experience of the Christmas Spirit. She was truly excited to celebrate the day with her family in love and joy. But what touches my heart most deeply and brings a smile to my face is the memory of hearing *"Do you think they're up yet?"* ❋

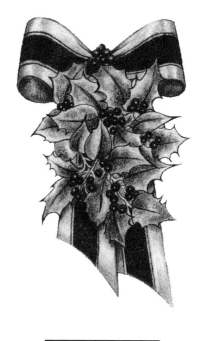

The essence of Christmas remained the same — the love, joy, togetherness and celebration.

Star

The star symbolizes the Star of the East, the sign that God had
provided the promised Saviour for all mankind.

Bows

A bow represents the sisterhood and brotherhood
that joins us together.

Candy Canes

A candy cane is shaped like the shepherd's crook used to help
bring stray sheep back to safety. It can remind us
to lend a helping hand at Christmas.

Christmas
MEMORIES

———————————

YEAR

Family & Friends
Who Visited

———————————————— ————————————————

———————————————— ————————————————

———————————————— ————————————————

———————————————— ————————————————

———————————————— ————————————————

———————————————— ————————————————

———————————————— ————————————————

———————————————— ————————————————

People We Visited

_____

_____

_____

_____

_____

_____

_____

FAMILY AND FRIENDS

Christmas Eve

The sights, sounds, tastes and celebrations

_____

_____

_____

_____

_____

_____

_____

Christmas Day

How We Spent Our Day

_____

_____

_____

_____

_____

_____

_____

_____

Who We Shared Christmas Dinner With

_____

_____

_____

_____

What Was Served

_____

_____

_____

_____

_____

_____

_____

_____

_____

_____

OUR FAVOURITE RECIPE

Our Home For The Holidays

_____

_____

_____

_____

_____

_____

_____

_____

_____

OUR DECORATED HOME

What Touched Our Hearts

Sights, sounds, events, people

_____

_____

_____

_____

_____

_____

Special Gifts

_____

_____

_____

_____

_____

What We Want To Remember
Memorable moments, future celebrations

A MEMORABLE MOMENT

Favourite Memories of Family and Friends

Christmas

These pages
are yours to use
as creatively as
you wish.

Memories

Plum Pudding

FEASTS HAVE LONG BEEN A PART
OF CHRISTMAS CELEBRATIONS.

PLUM PUDDING, one of the more famous traditional English dishes, often conjures up a Victorian Christmas image, even though many North Americans have never tasted it. Long before the first plum pudding was made, a dish made of hulled wheat boiled in milk and seasoned with spices, cinnamon and sugar was traditionally the first food eaten on Christmas morning in England. This became plum porridge as meat, eggs, rum, brandy and dried fruits such as raisins and currants were added. Around 1670 the first plum puddings, a thickened version of this porridge, were made. Interestingly, there were no plums in the recipe. The word "plum" once meant to rise or swell, so "plum pudding" may refer to the fact that the ingredients swelled during cooking.

On "Stir-up Sunday," the last Sunday before Advent, the entire family gathered and each member took a turn stirring the thick stew in the large copper kettle, while making a wish. Silver trinkets, coins or charms were sometimes added while stirring the pudding. "Stir-up Sunday" got its name from the prayer in the church service that day, which went "Stir up, we beseech thee, O Lord, the wills of thy faithful people; that they, plenteously bringing forth the fruit of good works …"

The plum pudding recipes common today, with fruits, nuts, alcohol and hard sauce, developed over time. The shape also changed from the traditional sphere to a pudding mold, which was more convenient. However, the plum pudding still arrives at the table ablaze with burning brandy, a reminder of the rebirth of the Son, and decorated with a sprig of holly, the symbol of everlasting life.✳

Plum Pudding

Plum pudding is the traditional Christmas dessert in my husband's family.
This recipe, generously donated by my sister-in-law Diane, has passed from one generation
to the next with each person adding their own personal touch.

Enjoy!

Plum Pudding

2 cups dark raisins
1 cup currants
1 cup chopped figs
1 1/2 cups chopped peel
1 cup glazed cherries
1/2 cup toasted silvered almonds
1 1/4 cups flour
1/2 tsp. salt
1/2 tsp. cinnamon
1/2 tsp. nutmeg
1/4 tsp. mace
1/4 tsp. cloves
1 1/2 cups bread crumbs
1 1/2 cups shredded suet
1 1/2 cups brown sugar
1/2 cup honey
4 beaten eggs
1 cup rum

Put the prepared fruits and almonds in a large bowl. Combine the flour, salt and spices in another bowl, add to the fruit mixture and mix well. Combine the remaining ingredients and mix well. Fill greased molds 2/3 full and cover tightly. Steam in a large pot for 5 hours. Allow to ripen in a cool place for at least 2 weeks. Heat the pudding before serving in a microwave on high for 5 minutes or steam for 1 hour. Serve with a hard sauce. Makes enough for two 2-quart molds.

Hard Sauce

What would plum pudding be without hard sauce to top it off!

1 cup sifted icing sugar
3 to 4 tbsp. butter
1/8 tsp. salt
1 tsp. vanilla.
1 egg

Beat the butter until soft. Gradually add the icing sugar and beat until well blended. Add the salt and vanilla. Stir. Beat in the egg. When the mixture is very smooth, chill thoroughly.

THE HISTORY OF
Mistletoe

THE CUSTOM of kissing under mistletoe came from a Scandinavian myth. One night Balder, the most loved of all the gods, dreamt danger was approaching. His mother, Frigga, bestowed upon him a charm that had been blessed by everything in the world that could possibly harm him. They all promised to keep him safe, and they kept their word. If a deadly object was thrown at Balder it would fall short or turn to the side. Loki, who was jealous of Balder, made an arrow from mistletoe, knowing that Frigga had overlooked this harmless plant. Loki gave the arrow to the blind Holder and helped him aim, so he could test out Balder's charm.

The mistletoe arrow hit Balder's heart and he died. Frigga, the goddess of love and beauty, blessed the plant in her grief, and declared it would be a symbol of love. It is said that the plant's white berries are Frigga's tears. All the gods helped to restore Balder to life. Extremely grateful for her son's return, Frigga promised to give anyone a kiss who passed under the mistletoe.

Mistletoe became the plant of peace in Scandinavia. If enemies met under the mistletoe they would lay down their weapons and call a truce until the next day. According to legend, any time a man kisses a woman under the mistletoe, he must pluck a white berry from it and give it to her. When there are no more berries, the mistletoe loses its power and there are no kisses left. ✳

Christmas
M E M O R I E S

_____

Family & Friends
Who Visited

_____ _____

_____ _____

_____ _____

_____ _____

_____ _____

_____ _____

_____ _____

_____ _____

People We Visited

_____

_____

_____

_____

_____

_____

FAMILY AND FRIENDS

Christmas Eve

The sights, sounds, tastes and celebrations

_____

_____

_____

_____

_____

_____

Christmas Day

How We Spent Our Day

_____
_____
_____
_____
_____
_____
_____
_____

Who We Shared Christmas Dinner With

_____
_____
_____
_____

OUR FAVOURITE RECIPE

What Was Served

_____
_____
_____
_____
_____
_____
_____
_____

Our Home For The Holidays

_____
_____
_____
_____
_____
_____
_____
_____
_____

OUR DECORATED HOME

What Touched Our Hearts
Sights, sounds, events, people

_____
_____
_____
_____
_____
_____

Special Gifts

_____
_____
_____
_____
_____
_____

What We Want To Remember
Memorable moments, future celebrations

A MEMORABLE MOMENT

Favourite Memories of Family and Friends

Christmas

These pages are yours to use as creatively as you wish.

Memories

THE HISTORY OF
Christmas Cards

CHRISTMAS CARDS OF THE EARLY 1870S
RESEMBLED VALENTINE'S CARDS.

BEFORE THE ADVENT of Christmas cards, adults exchanged written Christmas greetings in England and New Year's cards in Europe, and children gave their parents "Christmas pieces." These were specially decorated pieces of paper with Biblical or nature-scene borders. In the centre of the paper, schoolchildren wrote their parents a holiday wish to showcase their writing. In the early 19th century, two events led to the development of Christmas cards: the creation of the British penny post and the invention of the steam press.

Although it's not clear who developed the first Christmas card, credit is usually given to Henry Cole and John Horsley. Mr. Cole, who later became Sir Henry Cole, was the first director of the Victoria and Albert Museum in England. In 1843, Cole asked his friend John Horsley to design a card for Christmas. The card showed a family sipping wine, surrounded by trellis work. Two side panels depicted acts of charity and a central message proclaimed "A Merry Christmas and A Happy New Year to You." In 1846, one thousand copies were printed, hand-painted and then sold for a shilling each.

Three other people could qualify as the inventor of the first Christmas card. In 1844, Mr. W. Dobsen gave personally hand-painted Christmas cards to his friends and the Rev. Edward Bradley mailed out lithographed cards. The third claim, by William Egley, is difficult to assess as the last digit of the date on the card is unclear. For now, the generally accepted view is that Horsley and Cole created the Christmas card, since their cards were commercially sold.

Christmas cards became popular with the invention of the chromo-lithographic process. This resulted in cheap colour reproduction and brought the price of cards within reach of most people. In 1870, their popularity increased when the British Post Office introduced halfpenny postage for cards. By 1880, sending Christmas cards was so popular that the Post Office asked people to mail early for Christmas.

Christmas cards of the early 1870s resembled Valentine's cards. They were made by the same companies, often with the same picture on the card, and were decorated with lace, garlands of flowers, silk fringes, and satin or plush inserts. These pictures were soon replaced by more Christmas-oriented themes such as a snowy village, Christmas bells, a village church, children snowballing and ice skating. Cards with religious themes appeared later.

Although Christmas cards came to North America in the 1850s, it wasn't until 1875, when Louis Prang printed his first cards, that Christmas cards became popular here. Prang was a German-born printer living in Massachusetts. His Christmas cards, which first had floral designs and later changed to seasonal themes, were of the highest quality. Prang organized nation-wide competitions for Christmas card designs, awarding prizes for the best one. His efforts helped popularize Christmas cards in America. However, with the influx of cheaper cards from Europe in the 1890s, Prang found he could not compete and still maintain the quality, so he stopped printing Christmas cards.✳

Xmas

In the Greek language, X (the letter chi) is the first letter of Christ's name. In Greece, it has always stood as a symbol for Christ. Ironically, many people today feel it removes Christ from Christmas. The word "Xmas" has been used since the 12th century as a simple abbreviation for Christmas.

Christmas Colours

Red and green are considered the colours of Christmas, yet there is no definite reason for this choice. The most likely explanation is that they are the colours of holly, used in mid-winter celebrations. The deep green leaves symbolize everlasting life and the red berries symbolize Christ's blood. White is the traditional colour chosen by the church. Red and green are being replaced in many homes today by dark blue and silver, or red and gold.

THE HISTORY OF
Gift Giving

MID-WINTER GIFT-GIVING dates back to Roman times, when presents called strenae were exchanged during the festival of the Kalends on the first day of January. The Emperor Caligula proclaimed that he must be given gifts during the Kalends, then stood on his porch waiting to receive them. These early gifts were branches of evergreen picked from the grove of the Goddess of Strenia. Later, gifts represented wishes for the new year: honey was given for a year of sweetness, lamps for light, and silver or gold for wealth. This custom continues in France today, as bachelors give sweets to friends who have entertained them during the past year. When the church was unable to stop this pagan custom, it decreed that gifts would be given in the name of Jesus, God's gift to man. The Magi and St. Nicholas would be the gift bearers.

Today in many countries, gifts are secretly given to children between December 5, the Eve of St. Nicholas, and January 5, the Eve of Epiphany. Adults often exchange presents with family and friends on a different day. Some countries still follow traditional gift-giving customs, many of which seem to be based on the element of surprise and anonymity. In Holland, after dinner on Sinterklaas Eve, a basket of Sinterklaas (St. Nicholas) gifts is passed among the group. Each gift, accompanied by a witty, anonymous verse, has been imaginatively wrapped to disguise its contents. The recipient reads the amusing or embarrassing verse aloud before opening the gift. In Sweden, Christmas gifts, called Julklappur, come from the ancient custom of giving joke gifts anonymously. Gifts were delivered either by the giver, who knocked on the door and ran away leaving a wrapped gift, or by two masked figures, an old man ringing a bell and an old woman carrying a basket of presents.

When a gift is given to another, whether as part of a traditional custom or not, most people agree that it is the thought and care put into a gift that is truly important. A beautifully wrapped gift that has come from the heart will grace both giver and receiver with the pleasure and Spirit of Christmas.✳

Christmas

M E M O R I E S

———————————————

Y E A R

Family & Friends
Who Visited

_____ _____

_____ _____

_____ _____

_____ _____

_____ _____

_____ _____

_____ _____

_____ _____

People We Visited

_____

_____

_____

_____

_____

_____

_____

FAMILY AND FRIENDS

Christmas Eve

The sights, sounds, tastes and celebrations

_____

_____

_____

_____

_____

_____

_____

Christmas Day

How We Spent Our Day

_____
_____
_____
_____
_____
_____
_____
_____

Who We Shared Christmas Dinner With

_____
_____
_____
_____

OUR FAVOURITE RECIPE

What Was Served

_____
_____
_____
_____
_____
_____
_____
_____

Our Home For The Holidays

_____

_____

_____

_____

_____

_____

_____

_____

_____

OUR DECORATED HOME

What Touched Our Hearts

Sights, sounds, events, people

_____

_____

_____

_____

_____

Special Gifts

_____

_____

_____

_____

_____

What We Want To Remember
Memorable moments, future celebrations

A MEMORABLE MOMENT

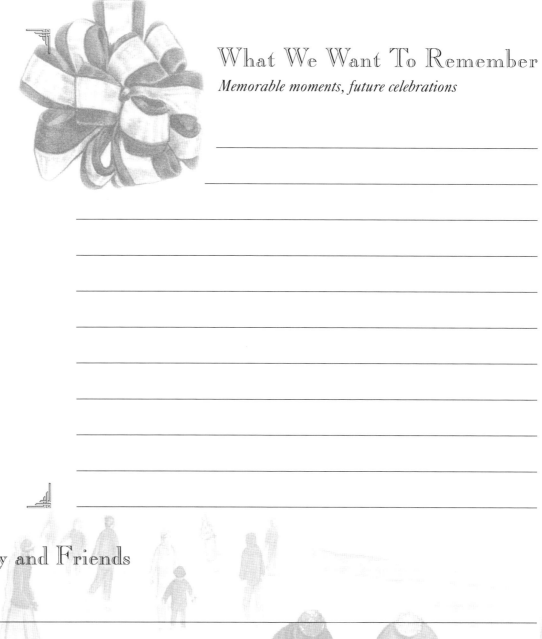

Favourite Memories of Family and Friends

Christmas

These pages are yours to use as creatively as you wish.

Memories

A Time of Gentleness

THE MILD COASTAL community I live in usually experiences no more than one day of snow a year and that snow generally melts within 24 hours. A few days before Christmas, 1996, it began to snow. This snow, which showed no sign of melting, stuck to trees, cars, the ground and people's clothing. As my husband and I drove around town, with snow lightly falling against the car, we thought how beautiful everything looked. The sun reflected off snow-covered branches, and brightly coloured lights shimmered on white roof tops. We breathed in the beauty and peacefulness of the freshly fallen snow as we travelled that day.

It snowed all that day and the next and the day after that. Six days after we saw the first snowflake, the ground was under several feet of snow. But the seventh night brought the largest amount yet. More than two feet of snow fell overnight and now a blizzard raged outside. Snow and ice pelted against our living room windows. Cars lay buried to their roofs and our landmarks were smothered by a blanket of white.

This final storm was more than the city could handle. Radio and television newscasts reported the city was closed to all except emergency vehicles. Cocooned, warm and safe by our fireplace, with the Christmas tree lights on and carols playing, we watched as the storm subsided that afternoon.

By the next afternoon I felt confined and wanted to be outside. With the seawalk under four feet of snow, I decided on a trip to the grocery store to replenish our post-Christmas fridge. Dressed in many layers, shopping bags in hand, I started out the front door. I stopped in astonishment at what I saw. Six-foot-high walls of snow hid the main road. Only a narrow trail dug through the snow lay in front of me. As I walked along this trail, not sure which way it would turn next, I felt like an explorer out to see the new world. Once I had successfully manoeuvred this winding trail I reached the lower, more packed snow of the side road. Then I had to climb over the five-foot snow bank flung up by the plows. When I reached the main road I did indeed feel like I had found a new world! The usually wide road was now two narrow bands of asphalt, with six-foot-high snow banks on either side. There were many people walking on the road and the occasional car.

It wasn't only the amount of snow that was so extraordinary, it was also the people's behaviour. Brought together by the snow, they were exchanging greetings and taking the time to talk with one another. There was energy and excitement in this friendly, social atmosphere. It felt like a winter carnival. When the occasional car went by, people either walked to the other side of the road or stood in knee-deep snow to let it pass. On that cold winter day I was struck by how warm and comforting it felt to be walking down the middle of the road with strangers. As I continued my journey by bus I saw people help each other by pushing or shovelling cars stuck in the snow.

After shopping, as I walked with a couple to the main road, we saw the bus go by. Since they knew the next bus wouldn't come for a long time, this kind couple offered me a ride. The residents of their building had worked together to clear a path to the main road for vehicles. How fortunate for all of us. As we shared the ride home I enjoyed the warmth of conversation, the coziness of the vehicle and the blanket of snow that made it possible. At their turnoff I got out, thanking them again for their generous kindness. I walked the last few blocks to our apartment, exchanging greetings with people I met and enjoying the social atmosphere. Once home I warmed my toes by the fire, told my husband of my adventure and reflected on all I had seen that day: the goodwill, compassion, generosity and kindness among people.

Four full days passed before the snow was plowed from our building to the main road. I later learned that much of the city had been closed during this time, shopping malls included. It was a time of gentleness, togetherness and humanity within our city. There are many stories of people getting to know each other and helping each other out. People gave supplies and food to those in need, shovelled driveways, dug cars out of the snow, and did errands for those who couldn't get out. Community was formed by this storm.

I believe our city was given a gift that winter, and I will always remember the kindness, compassion and joy I saw. Those four snowed-in days were a true celebration of life and the human spirit.❊

Christmas
MEMORIES

_____

YEAR

Family & Friends
Who Visited

_____ _____

_____ _____

_____ _____

_____ _____

_____ _____

_____ _____

_____ _____

_____ _____

People We Visited

_____

_____

_____

_____

_____

_____

FAMILY AND FRIENDS

Christmas Eve
The sights, sounds, tastes and celebrations

_____

_____

_____

_____

_____

_____

_____

_____

Christmas Day

How We Spent Our Day

_____

_____

_____

_____

_____

_____

_____

_____

_____

Who We Shared Christmas Dinner With

_____

_____

_____

_____

What Was Served

_____

_____

_____

_____

_____

_____

_____

_____

_____

Our Home For The Holidays

_____
_____
_____
_____
_____
_____
_____
_____
_____
_____

OUR DECORATED HOME

What Touched Our Hearts
Sights, sounds, events, people

_____
_____
_____
_____
_____
_____

Special Gifts

_____
_____
_____
_____
_____
_____

What We Want To Remember

Memorable moments, future celebrations

A MEMORABLE MOMENT

_____

_____

_____

_____

_____

_____

_____

_____

_____

_____

_____

_____

Favourite Memories of Family and Friends

_____

_____

_____

_____

_____

_____

_____

_____

Christmas

These pages
are yours to use
as creatively as
you wish.

Memories

The Ceremony of Light

O VER THE PAST fifteen years my husband Mark and I have celebrated Christmas in many different cities. Each city has its own set of memories, smiles, laughter and events that touched my heart. One of my fondest Christmas memories is from our time in Toronto. After moving there, we soon discovered the area we lived in, called The Beach by some and The Beaches by others, was a community all to itself. Along the main street were banks, restaurants, grocery stores, clothing stores, a toy store and a library. Like the other residents, we could walk everywhere from our home and did most of our shopping and errands on foot. Retailers would wave to "the regulars" as they walked by, and people would stop and talk with one another on the street. The community glowed with a warm, friendly atmosphere. *Continued next page.*

Outdoor Christmas Lights

The first outdoor tree lights were the result of a little boy's
wish. As he watched his family decorate their Christmas tree
from his sick bed, he pointed outside and said,
"Daddy, I wish you could put lights on that tree out there."
His father thought for a moment and found a way
to fulfil his son's wish.

Candles

A candle flame symbolizes man's gratitude for the birth of
the infant Christ who was considered "The Light of the
World." Although Christmas trees were originally decorated
with candles to represent the Star that appeared to
announce the birth, today coloured tree lights fill this role.

A LARGE PARK that stretched from the main road down to the lakefront was the venue for many activities and special events throughout the year. In July there was a lively jazz festival and in August relaxing music on Sunday afternoons. But the best event was in December — the glorious ceremony of light!

One year, bundled up against the early December snow, we walked to the park for the ceremony. As we approached, bright colours flashed from children's coats, hats, and mitts as they darted in between the adults. We were given candles and song sheets, and offered hot drinks to ward off the chill. The park filled with people and finally the time came to light the tree. In an instant the red, yellow, blue and green lights twinkled among the snowy branches. The crowd fell silent. We breathed in the beauty before us and each in turn extended a candle to light a neighbour's. As the glow of candlelight spread throughout the group we sang "Silent Night." Peacefulness and warmth enveloped us.

After singing many Christmas carols, we ended with "Santa Claus Is Coming To Town." On the last words, we heard a clamour up on the street. Within moments Santa Claus appeared, not with eight reindeer, but riding a fire truck! He jumped off the truck, greeted people and handed out candy canes to the children. Then, with a "Merry Christmas!" he sprang back aboard, and with a wave, vanished into the dark night.

The park emptied as people exchanged holiday wishes and returned home, rejoicing in the Christmas Spirit. For the rest of the Christmas season the evergreen tree remained lit — a symbol of fellowship and ceremony. It was like a beacon, reminding us of the hope, love and beauty that surrounds us during this season. And every year I remember that community that chose to gather in celebration of Christmas.✳

Christmas
MEMORIES

_____

YEAR

Family & Friends
Who Visited

_____   _____

_____   _____

_____   _____

_____   _____

_____   _____

_____   _____

_____   _____

_____   _____

_____   _____

People We Visited

_____

_____

_____

_____

_____

_____

_____

FAMILY AND FRIENDS

Christmas Eve

The sights, sounds, tastes and celebrations

_____

_____

_____

_____

_____

_____

_____

Christmas Day

How We Spent Our Day

_____
_____
_____
_____
_____
_____
_____
_____
_____

Who We Shared Christmas Dinner With

_____
_____
_____
_____

OUR FAVOURITE RECIPE

What Was Served

_____
_____
_____
_____
_____
_____
_____
_____
_____

Our Home For The Holidays

_____
_____
_____
_____
_____
_____
_____
_____
_____
_____

OUR DECORATED HOME

What Touched Our Hearts

Sights, sounds, events, people

_____
_____
_____
_____
_____
_____

Special Gifts

_____
_____
_____
_____
_____

What We Want To Remember

Memorable moments, future celebrations

A MEMORABLE MOMENT

_____

_____

_____

_____

_____

_____

_____

_____

_____

_____

_____

Favourite Memories of Family and Friends

_____

_____

_____

_____

_____

_____

_____

_____

_____

Christmas

These pages
are yours to use
as creatively as
you wish.

Memories

Christmas
M E M O R I E S

Karen Culos ~ Writer

FASCINATED BY THE instruments of this art — fountain pens and beautiful stationery — Karen began writing at an early age. Poems, plays, short stories and volumes of letters flowed from the creativity of her young imagination. *Christmas Memories*, her first book, is an expression of her constant seeking for the joy in life. When she is not writing, Karen facilitates workshops that assist people in living their lives passionately and purposefully. After living in many cities and travelling extensively, Karen and her husband Mark now call Victoria home.

Maria Miranda Lawrence ~ Artist (paintings)

AS A YOUNG CHILD growing up in Kitimat, Maria's favorite pastime was drawing, which quickly grew into a passion. Formally trained at the Kootenay School of Art, she has continued to study and develop her talent over the past twenty-four years. Working with paint, pencil or clay to capture the subtleties of the human experience is her first love; sharing her enthusiasm for art and encouraging others to explore their artistic abilities comes a close second. Maria lives in Victoria with her husband Jim and their two daughters Corinne and Kara.

Linda Leadbetter ~ Artist (drawings)

WHETHER IN KELOWNA or Edmonton, pencils and pastels were natural extensions of Linda's hand through her formative years. Her love of art led to a career in commissioned portraiture that culminated in her last and most significant piece: her own wedding invitation. The joys of family life have over the past ten years superceded Linda's art career and *Christmas Memories* marks her triumphant return. Home for Linda is in Victoria with her husband David and daughters Chelsea and Brittany.

Christmas
MEMORIES

Bibliography

Cooke, Gillian, and Fordham, David, *A Celebration of Christmas*,
G.P. Putnam and Sons, New York, 1980.

Del Re, Gerard and Patricia, *The Christmas Almanack*,
Doubleday and Company Inc, Garden City, 1979.

Hottes, Alfred Carl, *1001 Christmas Facts and Fancies*,
A.T. De La Mare Company, Inc., New York, 1937.

Ickis, Marguerite, *Book of Religious Holidays and Celebrations*,
Dodd, Mead and Company, New York, 1966.

Muir, Frank, *Christmas Customs and Traditions*,
Taplinger Publishing Co. Inc., New York, 1975.

Thomas, Dian, *Holiday Fun Year Round*,
The Dian Thomas Company, Holladay, Utah, 1995.